Will Rogers Says...

Favorite Quotations
Selected by the Memorial Staff

Will Rogers Says...

Favorite Quotations
Selected by the Will Rogers Memorial Staff

Edited by
Dr. Reba Collins

Selections by
Gregory N. Malak, Manager
Patricia A. Lowe, Librarian
and Dr. Reba Collins, Director Emeritus
of the Will Rogers Memorial and Research Center

Neighbors and Quaid, Inc.
Oklahoma City, Oklahoma
1993

Born November 4, 1879, in Indian Territory — near present Oologah, Oklahoma — William Penn Adair Rogers was the eighth and last child of Clement Vann and Mary America Schrimsher Rogers. Both were about one-quarter Cherokee and Will was always proud of his Cherokee heritage.

His formal schooling was sketchy, but he continued to learn throughout his life as he traveled the world in show business, dined with kings and presidents, swapped "gags" with famous writers and performers, and devoured what he read "in the papers."

Over a half-million visitors a year come to the Memorial in Claremore to see the mementoes of his life, to read some of the two million words he wrote, to view the films in which he starred and to pay tribute at his tomb. (Rogers was killed in a plane crash near Barrow, Alaska, August 15, 1935.)

Just 10 miles away on Lake Oologah is the Dog Iron Ranch — Birthplace of Will Rogers. No drug-store cowboy, Will rode and roped on the range where they ran up to 10,000 head of cattle.

Here you find the roots of his down-to-earth humor and his zest for living life to the fullest, the brilliant blue skies that were reflected in his twinkling blue eyes, and his shy charm that was as open and honest as the great Oklahoma prairie.

"Will Rogers was the greatest communicator America ever produced." So said Dr. Laurence Peter when he dedicated the Research Center at the Will Rogers Memorial in Claremore, Oklahoma, in 1982.

"Rogers excelled in every field of communication that existed during his lifetime. He was tops at the box office in his last years, the most widely read newspaper columnist, highest paid radio commentator, favorite of stage producers, a roper without peer, and everyone's favorite after-dinner speaker. No one living can measure up to that example," added the noted Peter-Principle-Man.

Staff members at the Will Rogers Memorial and Research Center readily agree. Even though we have read his writings — examined his "sayings" over and over again through the years — we still chuckle, sometimes laugh out loud as we stumble across a choice bit and suddenly see it in a new light....

"Listen to this," someone will say. And we all share in wonder at his wit and his wisdom. That is why we decided to do this book...to share our favorite quotations with others.

Over a period of years, professional members of the Memorial staff have selected their favorites — over 2,000, all told. A committee of "readers" then made final selections for this publication.

We hope you too will enjoy what Will Rogers said.

Dr. Reba Collins, Director Emeritu
Will Rogers Memorial and Research Cente

Contents

The Will Rogers Memorial,
Claremore, Oklahoma,
was dedicated
November 4, 1938.

What's This Country Coming To

We are not the whole of America, we are just a part of the U.S. of North America.

ML: Feb. 27, 1932

It always will seem funny to us United Staters that we are about the only ones that really know how to do everything right. I don't know how a lot of these other Nations have existed as long as they have till we could get some of our people around and show 'em really how to be Pure and Good like us.

ML: Feb. 27, 1932

Americans are getting like a Ford car — they all have the same parts, the same upholstering and all make exactly the same noises.

DTI: Oct. 20, 1926

You give us long enough to argue over something and we will bring you in proofs to show that the Ten Commandments should never be ratified.

DTII: Apr. 14, 1930

America and Russia are the only two countries left in the world with any scheme of life. Russia is trying an experiment, and America is trying everything.

DTII: Jul. 27, 1930

1

America has a unique record. We never lost a war and we never won a conference in our lives.

RB: Apr. 6, 1930

America is a land of opportunity and don't ever forget it.

DTIII: Jul. 1, 1934

Geography has been mighty good to us. It's wonderful to pay honor to Washington and Lincoln, but I want to tell you we ought to lay out one day a year for the old boy that laid out the location of this country. I don't know who he was, but boy he was a sage, that bird was.

RB: Apr. 6, 1930

Headlines in papers say: "Europe criticises U.S." If memory serves me right we haven't complimented them lately ourselves.

WAI: Jan. 27, 1924

YOU CAN TAKE A SOB STORY AND A STICK OF CANDY AND LEAD AMERICA RIGHT OFF INTO THE DEAD SEA.

WAI: Dec. 2, 1932

Never in our history was we as willing to blame somebody else for our troubles.

DTIV: Apr. 28, 1932

Every town should have some kind of yearly celebration. Didn't Rome have its annual bathing festival?

So think up something for your town to celebrate. Have a parade. Americans like to parade. We are a parading nation. "Upluribus paraditorious" (some paraders).

DTIII: Aug. 18, 1932

2

We don't have to worry about anything. No nation in the history of the world was ever sitting as pretty. If we want anything, all we have to do is go and buy it on credit.

DTI: Sep. 6, 1928

We are a great people to get tired of anything awful quick. We just jump from one extreme to another.

HT: Mar. 30, 1929

This country is not where it is today on account of any man. It is here on account of the big normal majority.

WAI: Feb. 22, 1925

When an Office Holder, or one that has been found out, can't think of anything to deliver a speech on, he always falls back on the good old subject, AMERICANISM.

WAI: Feb. 22, 1925

We can get hot and bothered quicker over nothing, and cool off faster than any nation in the world.

DTII: Feb. 13, 1930

Us middle class...never have to worry about having old furniture to point out to our friends. We buy it on payments and before it's paid for it's plenty antique.

DTII: Oct. 9, 1930

For the American people are a very generous people and will forgive almost any weakness, with the possible exception of stupidity.

WAI: Feb. 24, 1924

Every invention during our lifetime has been just to save time, and time is the only commodity that every American, both rich and poor, has plenty of. Half our life is spent trying to find something to do with the time we have rushed through life trying to save. Two hundred years from now history will record "America, a nation that flourished from 1900 to 1942, conceived many odd inventions for getting somewhere, but could think of nothing to do when they got there."

DTII: Apr. 28, 1930

You know no Nation has a monopoly on good things, each one has something that the others could well afford to adopt.

WAIV: Nov. 30, 1930

People are marvelous in their generosity if they just know the cause is there...

DTIII: Jun. 10, 193.

Here we go again! America is running true to form, fixing some other country's business for 'em just as we always do. We mean well, but will wind up in wrong as usual.

DTIII: Jun. 22, 193

No nation ever had two better friends than we have. You know who they are. Well they are the Atlantic and Pacific ocean.

WAVI: Apr. 9, 193.

There is two things that tickle the fancy of our citizens, one is let him act on a committee, and the other is promise him to let him walk in a parade.

What America needs is to get more mileage out of our parades.

DTII: Sep. 1, 192

My Ancestors
Dident Come Over
on the Mayflower,
but They Met 'em at the Boat

My own mother died when I was ten years old. My folks have told me that what little humor I have comes from her. I can't remember her humor but I can remember her love and understanding of me. Of course, the mother I know the most about is the mother of our little group. She has been for twenty-two years trying to raise to maturity four children, three by birth and one by marriage. While she hasn't done a good job, the poor soul has done all that mortal human could do with the material she had to work with.

RB: May 11, 1930

...Ireland. That is where some of my folks come from. There is a fine breed for you, Irish-Indian. Ziegfeld says I have a touch of Hebraic in me, too. Which would make me an Irish, Jewish, Indian.

My family crest would in that case be, a Shillalah with a Tomahawk on one end, and a percent sign (%) on the other.

WAI: Nov. 30, 1924

I am mighty happy I am going home to my own people, who know me as "Willie, Uncle Clem Rogers' boy who wouldn't go to school but just kept running around the country throwing a

5

rope, till I think he finally got in one of them shows." They don't know how I make a living. They just know me as Uncle Clem's boy. They are my real friends and when no one else will want to hear my measly old jokes, I want to go home. It won't make no difference to them.

WAI: May 25, 1924

...I don't think I ever hurt any man's feelings by my little gags. I know I never willfully did it. When I have to do that to make a living I will quit.

WAI: Aug. 19, 1923

I am just an old country boy in a big town trying to get along. I have been eating pretty regular, and the reason I have been is because I have stayed an old country boy.

WAI: Aug. 31, 1924

Ah, folks, you can act, and talk, and do stunts, all over the world, but the applause of a home audience is sweeter to your ears than anything in the world.

DTII: Apr. 22, 1930

I think that early morning, say from seven to eight, was meant for sleeping. That's when I do all my heavy thinking — is when I am sleeping from seven to eight A.M.

ML: Feb. 27, 1932

*From typewriter to linotype,
Will Rogers plays the role
of a small-town publisher.*

Promise Everything,
Deliver Nothing

Politics and Politicians

You know the platform will always be the same, promise everything, deliver nothing.

WAIII Jul. 8, 1928

This country has gotten where it is in spite of politics, not by the aid of it.

DTIII: Nov. 1, 1932

One of the evils of democracy is you have to put up with the man you elect whether you want him or not. That's why we call it democracy.

DTIII: Nov. 7, 1932

With every public man we have elected doing comedy, I tell you I don't see much of a chance for a comedian to make a living. I am just on the verge of going to work. They can do more funny things naturally, than I can think of to do purposely.

WAI: Jan. 13, 1924

Will Rogers and Shirley Temple share honors as top box office stars in 1934.

9

On account of us being a democracy and run by the people, we are the only nation in the world that has to keep a government four years no matter what it does.

DTII: Feb. 21, 1930

Politics is a great character builder. You have to take a referendum to see what your convictions are for that day.

DTII: May 29, 1930

That's the trouble with a Politician's life somebody is always interrupting it with an election.

WAI: unpublished

A smart state nowadays will appoint all their highway men from one place. Then one road will do all of 'em.

WAIV: Feb. 2, 1930

A Politican is just like a spoiled Kid. If he feels that his stick of candy is not the longest why he will let out a yap that will drown out the neighborhood.

WAIV: Aug. 17, 1930

Lord, the money we do spend on Government. And it's not a bit better government than we got for one-third the money twenty years ago.

WAV: Mar. 27, 1932

Anyhow, how can you tell when a Vice President makes good and when he don't. They have never given one anything to do yet to find out.

CA: Jun. 13, 1932

Slogan: Be a politician; no training necessary.

WAII: Apr. 12, 1925

Any audience who would gather to hear a politican speak wouldn't know a good speech if they heard one.

RB: Apr. 27, 1930

There is nothing that a Vice President can do but be a Vice President. You take that title away from him and he can't hand you a Card.

HT: Mar. 30, 1929

Imagine a man in public office that everybody knew where he stood. We wouldn't call him a statesman, we would call him a curiosity.

DTIII: Mar. 1, 1933

Make every speaker, as soon as he tells all he knows, sit down. That will shorten your speeches so much you will be out by lunch time every day.

CA: Jun. 28, 1924

What this country needs is more working men and fewer politicans.

WAI: Oct. 5, 1924

Never blame a legislative body for not doing something. When they do nothing, that don't hurt anybody. It's when they do something is when they become dangerous.

DTII: Nov. 22, 1929

They say hot air rises. And I guess it does. An airplane flying over the Capitol the other day caught fire from outside sources.

WAI: Jan. 27, 1924

I wish America could get some of the political bandits that live off this country to come in and give up. Then we would know just what we were paying them to live on, instead of the present system of letting them grab what they can.

WAI: Aug. 5, 1923

A statesman is a man that can do what the politician would like to do but can't, because he is afraid of not being elected.

DTIV: Jul 5, 1934

If we could just send the same bunch of men to Washington for the good of the nation, and not for political reasons, we could have the most perfect government in the world.

WAI: Jun. 8, 1924

Politics ain't worrying this country one tenth as much as parking space.

WAI: Jan. 6, 1924

Ain't it funny how many hundreds of thousands of soldiers we can recruit with nerve. But we just can't find one politician in a million with backbone.

DTI: Feb. 18, 1929

I joke about our prominent men, but at heart I believe in 'em. I do think there is times when traces of "dumbness" crop up in official life, but not crookedness.

DTII: Mar. 18, 1930

But a politician is just like a pickpocket; it's almost impossible to get one to reform.

WAI: Mar. 25, 1923

You know yourself that about all there is to Politics is trading anyway.

ML: Jun. 2, 1928

In this country people don't vote for; they vote against.

RB: Jun. 9, 1935

When you straddle a thing it takes a long time to explain it.

CA: Jun. 29, 1924

They overestimate this Governor thing anyhow. States have good ones, bad ones and every kind, and yet they drag along about the same. Things in our country run in spite of government. Not by the aid of it.

DTII: Jul. 28, 1930

I am to go into Ziegfeld's new Follies, and I have no act. So I thought I will run down to Washington and get some material. Most people and actors appearing on the stage have some writer to write their material...but Congress is good enough for me. They have been writing my material for years.

WAI: Jun. 8, 1924

Once a man wants to hold a Public office he is absolutely no good for honest work.

WAII: Mar. 22, 1925

There's nothing will upset a state economic condition like a legislature. It's better to have termites in your house than the legislature.

RB: Mar. 31, 1935

Investigations

I have found out that when newspapers knock a man a lot, there is sure to be a lot of good in him.

WAI: Apr. 15, 1923

13

Well, what's the use of having a lot of statistics and data on something that you can't do — well, it's like garbage: What's the use of collecting it if you ain't got nowhere to put it; you don't know what to do with it. Well, that's the way with commissions.

RB: Apr. 30, 1933

You can't believe a thing you read in regard to official Statements. The minute anything happens connected with official life, why it's just like a cold night, everybody is trying to cover up.

WAII: Oct. 4, 1925

Statistics have proven that the surest way to get anything out of the public mind and never hear of it again is to have a Senate Committee appointed to look into it.

WAI: Feb. 10, 1924

They ought to pass a rule in this country in any investigations, if a man couldn't tell the truth the first time he shouldn't be allowed to try again.

WAI: Mar. 2, 1924

Presidents

A man don't any more than learn where the Ice Box is in the White House than he has to go back to being a lawyer again.

WAI: Nov. 11, 1923

Politics is the only sporting events in the world where they don't pay off for second money; a man to run second in any other event in the world it's an honor. But any time he runs second for President it's not an honor; it's a pity.

HT: Oct. 29, 1927

I honestly believe there is people so excited over this election that they think the President has something to do with running this country.

DTIII: Oct. 30, 1932

The high office of President of the United States has degenerated into two ordinarily fine men being goaded on by their political leeches into saying things that if they were in their right minds they wouldn't think of saying.

DTIII: Nov. 1, 1932

Harding was the most human of any of our late Presidents. There was more of the real "every day man" in him. If he had a weakness it was in trusting friends, and the man that don't do that, then there is something the matter with him sho nuff.

Betrayed by friendship is not a bad memorial to leave.

DTIII: Jun. 16, 1931

Now, if I was a President and wanted something I would claim I didn't want it. For Congress has not given any President anything that he wanted in the last 10 years. Be against anything and then he is sure to get it.

WAI: May 5, 1923

Now, take George Washington...he was a politician and a gentleman — that is a rare combination.

RB: Jun. 1, 1930

Coolidge is the first president to discover that what the American people want is to be let alone.

WAI: Jan. 27, 1924

[President Franklin D.] Roosevelt made a good speech yesterday and he gave aviation the biggest boost it ever had. Took his

15

family and flew out there. That will stop these big shots from thinking their lives are too important to the country to take a chance on flying.

DTIII: Jul. 3, 1932

We are a funny people. We elect our Presidents, be they Republcan or Democrat, then go home and start daring 'em to make good.

DTIV: Apr. 1, 1935

We shouldn't elect a President; we should elect a magician.

DTII: May 26, 1930

The last few days I have read various addresses made on Lincoln's Birthday. Every Politician always talks about him, but none of them every imitate him.

WAI: Feb. 22, 1925

You know it's remarkable the hold that little fellow (Coolidge) has on the people. They sure do believe in him. They know that he didn't do anything when in there. But he does nothing just at the time when the people want nothing done.

WAIV: Mar. 9, 1930

Coolidge kept his mouth shut. That was such a novelty among Politicians that it just swept the Country. Funny we never had another one to think of that before. You see originality will be rewarded in any line.

WAI: Nov. 16, 1924

Being serious, or being a good fellow, has got nothing to do with running this country, if the breaks are with you, you could be a laughing hyena and still have a great administration.

DTII: Oct. 10, 1930

This would be a great time in the world for some man to come along that knew something.

DTIII: Sep. 21, 1931

I don't know who started the idea that a President must be a Politician instead of a Business man. A Politician can't run any other kind of business. So there is no reason why he can run the U.S. That's the biggest single business in the World.

WAI: Jan. 21, 1923

Congressmen and Senators

Well, you know how Congress is. They'll vote for anything if the thing they vote for will turn around and vote for them.

RB: Jun. 2, 1935

Washington, D.C. papers say: "Congress is deadlocked and can't act." I think that is the greatest blessing that could befall this country.

WAI: Jan. 27, 1924

I suggested a plan one time to shorten the Senate debate. Every time a Senator tells all he knows, make him sit down. That will shorten it. Some of them wouldn't be able to answer roll call.

RB: Apr. 27, 1930

Well, all our Senators and Congressmen are away from Washington now. This is the season of the year when they do the least damage to their country. They are scattering all over the nation. Some are going to Europe, some even to Turkey. A Senator or a Congressman will go anywhere in the world to keep from going back home and facing his people after that last Congress.

WAI: Mar. 25, 1923

You see they have two of these bodies — Senate and Congress. That is for the convenience of visitors. If there is nothing funny happening in one there is sure to be in the other, and in case one body passes a good bill, why the other can see it in time, and kill it.

WAI: Jun. 8, 1924

The Senate has furnished more officeholders and less Presidents than any industry we have.

HT: May 1, 1926

What does the Senate do with all the knowledge they demand from other people? They never seem to use it.

DTII: Jun. 12, 1930

A Senator is never as happy as when he is asking somebody a question without the party being able to ask him one back.

WAIV: Nov. 24, 1929

The things about my jokes is they don't hurt anybody. You can take 'em or leave 'em. You know what I mean. You know, you say, well they're funny, or they're terrible, or they're good, or whatever it is, but they don't do any harm. You can just pass them by. But with Congress, every time they make a joke it's a law. You know. And every time they make a law it's a joke.

RB: May 12, 1935

They Go in on Promises and Come out on Alabis

Well the election will be breaking out pretty soon, and a flock of Democrats will replace a mess of Republicans in quite a few districts. It won't mean a thing, they will go in like all the rest of 'em, go in on promises and come out on Alabi's.

WAIV: Sep. 14, 1930

You got to be funny to be a Democrat. It takes more humor to be a Democrat than it does a Republican anyhow.

RB: Apr. 27, 1930

One thing you got to say for an administration that tries out a lot of plans, some of 'em are apt to be pretty good.

DTIV: Jun. 27, 1935

Naturally Parties always try to nominate somebody [for vice president] that you wouldent mind being seen with.

HT: p. 107, Jun. 1929

Talk about our civilization! Why, if they ever took a sanity test at a political convention 98 per cent would be removed to an asylum.

CA: Jun. 27, 1924

A convention is the only thing in the world, outside of the appendix, that no one has ever found a reason for. They generally arrive with the heat, and they are all the more mysterious when we figure that most of the attendants at them have left comfortable homes, and some even a business, to travel, shove, and sweat, all for the sake of wearing a badge.

HT: p. 148

You take a Democrat and a Republican and you keep them both out of office and I bet you they will turn out to be good friends and maybe make useful citizens, and devote their time to some work instead of lectioneering all the time.

WAI: Nov. 11, 1923

I have not aligned myself with any party. I am just sitting tight waiting for an attractive offer...

WAI: Nov. 11, 1923

I generally give the party in power, whether Republican or Democrat, the more digs because they are generally doing the country more damage, and besides I don't think it is fair to jump too much on the fellow who is down. He is not working, he is only living in hopes of getting back in on the graft in another four years, while the party in power is drawing a salary to be knocked.

WAI: Nov. 9, 1924

The Republicans mopped up, the Democrats gummed up, and I will now try and sum up. Things are terrible dull now. We won't have any more comedy until Congress meets. That's the next serious drama with funny lines.

WAI: Nov. 16, 1924

But I must get back from these political parties and get back to civilization, for there's nothing in common between politics and civilization.

RB: Apr. 14, 1935

Now everybody in the world gets hungry at some time or other but no animal in the world gets quite as hungry as a Democrat.

WAI: Aug. 10, 1924

You can't beat an Administration by attacking it. You have to show some plan of improving on it.

WAI: Nov. 16, 1924

You know it takes nerve to be a Democrat. But it takes money to be a Republican.

WAIII: Feb. 10, 1929

Democrats are attacking and the Republicans are defending. All the Democrats have to do is promise "what they would do if they got in." But the Republicans have to promise "what they would do" and then explain why they haven't already "done it."

DTIII: Sep. 26, 1932

There is one thing about a Democrat: He would rather make a Speech than a Dollar.

HT: Mar. 30, 1929

The whole trouble with the Republicans is their fear of an increase in income tax, especially on higher incomes. They speak of it almost like a national calamity. I really believe if it come to a vote whether to go to war with England, France and Germany combined, or raise the rate on incomes of over $100,000, they would vote war.

DTII: Feb. 27, 1931

You know the more you read and observe about this Politics thing, you got to admit that each party is worse than the other. The one that's out always looks the best.

WAI: Dec. 31, 1922

The Rich Get Rich and
The Poor Get Poorer

Taxes

There is a tremendous movement on to get lower taxes on earned incomes. Then will come the real problem. "Who among us on salary are earning our income?

DTII: Dec. 8, 1929

The idea that a tax on something keeps anybody from buying it is a lot of "hooey." They put it on gasoline all over the country and it hasn't kept a soul at home a single night or day. You could put a dollar a gallon on and still a pedestrian couldn't cross the street with safety without armor.

DTIII: Mar. 17, 1932

A tax paid on the day you buy is not as tough as asking you for it the next year when you are broke.

DTIII: Sep. 7, 1931

Well, as I go to press, everybody is on a trip somewhere if they work for the government. I wonder when the taxpayers take their trip.

WAI: Jul. 8, 1923

*All "slicked up," Will Rogers
emcees the Academy Awards banquet.*

23

(The income tax has made more liars out of the American people than golf has.)

Even when you make one out on the level, you don't know when it's through if you are a crook or a martyr.

WAI: Apr. 8, 1923

We will never get anywhere with our finances till we pass a law saying that every time we appropriate something we got to pass another bill along with it stating where the money is coming from.

DTIII: Feb. 12, 1932

It's a great country but you can't live in it for nothing.

DTIV: Feb. 6, 1934

Well, the good old days with most of us was when we didn't earn enough to pay an income tax.

DTIV: Mar. 31, 1935

It ain't taxes that is hurting this country; it's interest.

WAI: Jan. 6, 1924

When a party can't think of anything else they always fall back on Lower Taxes. It has a magic sound to a voter, just like Fairyland is spoken of and dreamed of by all children. But no child has ever seen it; neither has any voter ever lived to see the day when his taxes were lowered.

WAI: Oct. 19, 1924

Presidents have been promising lower taxes since Washington crossed the Delaware by hand in a row boat. But our taxes have gotten bigger and their boats have gotten larger until now the President crosses the Delaware in his private yacht.

WAI: Oct. 19, 1924

I wanted to get to see those Head Hunters you all have in your Country; we have 'em over Home, but we call 'em Income Tax Collectors.

ML: Apr. 30, 1932

Taxation is about all there is to Government....People want JUST taxes, more than they want lower taxes. They want to know that every man is paying his proportionate share according to his wealth.

WAI: Nov. 2, 1924

There's no income tax in Russia, but there's no income.

RB: Apr. 7, 1935

Depression

Depression ain't nothing but old man interest just gnawing away at us.

DTIII: Feb. 7, 1933

All Doctors should make enough out of those who are well able to pay, to be able to do all work for the poor free. That is one thing that a poor person should never be even expected to pay for is medical attention, and not from an organized Charity, but from our best Doctors. But your Doctor bill should be paid like your Income tax, according to what you have. There is nothing that keeps poor people poor as much as paying Doctor bills.

WAIV: Jul. 13, 1930

Don't make the first payment on anything. First payments is what made us think we were prosperous, and the other nineteen is what showed us we were broke.

DTII: Jul. 9, 1930

We'll hold the distinction of being the only nation in the history of the world that ever went to the poor house in an automobile.

RB: Oct. 18, 1931

Why don't somebody print the truth about our present economic situation? We spent six years of wild buying on credit (everything under the sun, whether we needed it or not) and now we are having to pay for 'em under Mr. Hoover, and we are howling like a pet coon.

P.S. This would be a great world to dance in if we didn't have to pay the fiddler.

DTII: Jun. 27, 1930

The world ain't going to be saved by nobody's scheme. It's fellows with schemes that got us into this mess. Plans get you into things, but you got to work your way out.

DTIII: Jun. 24, 1931

Stock Market

It's all right to let Wall Street bet each other millions of dollars every day but why make these bets effect the fellow who is plowing a field out in Claremore, Oklahoma.

WAI: Nov. 23, 1924

"Don't gamble"; take all your savings and buy some good stock, and hold it till it goes up, then sell it.

If it don't go up, don't buy it.

DTII: Oct. 31, 1929

But I am telling them that the Country as a whole is "Sound," and that all those who's heads are solid are bound to get back into the market again. I tell 'em that this Country is bigger than Wall Street, and if they don't believe it, I show 'em the map.

WAIV: Dec. 1, 1929

We are living in an age of "Mergers" and "Combines." When your business is not doing good you combine with something and sell more stock.

WAIV: Mar. 23, 1930

Business and Economics

If I wanted to put an object on the market today I would advertise, "It will last until it is paid for." Nothing could be better than that.

RB: Jun. 1, 1930

Every official in the Government and every prominent manufacturer is forever bragging about our "high standard of living." Why, we could always have lived this high if we had wanted to live on the instalment plan.

DTI: Dec. 9, 1926

All this Open-Door stuff is a lot of Hooey. Any Door is only open to those that have the best product at the cheapest money.

ML: Apr. 30, 1932

People that pay for things never complain. It's the guy you give something to that you can't please.

WAII: Jan. 3, 1926

Insurance companies have Guys figure out the very day you will die. (In fact they won't insure till they have it investigated and

27

find out.) Then you like a Sucker go bet them you will live longer than that.

WAIII: Feb. 24, 1929

Machines are a great thing, but if one replaces a hundred men, it don't buy anything, it don't eat anything, while the hundred men spend theirs back for food, shelter, and hundreds of various commodities for them and their families.

WAV: Sep. 6, 1931

An economist is a man that can tell you anything about — he'll tell you what can happen under any given conditions, and his guess is liable to be just as good as anybody else's, too.

RB: May 26, 1935

Farms

Farmers are learning that the relief they get from the sky beats what they get from Washington.

DTIV: Jun. 4, 1934

Our Foreign Dealings
Are an Open Book,
Generally a Check Book

Foreign Relations

There's the one thing no nation can ever accuse us of and that is
Secret Diplomacy. Our foreign dealings are an Open Book,
generally a Check Book.

WAI: Oct. 21, 1923

Nations are just like individuals. Loan them money and you lose
their friendship.

WAI: Jan. 11, 1925

A Russian just loves misery, and he wants to get as many in on it
as he can. He wants to share it among friends as well as foes.

WAIV: Dec. 28, 1930

That's one good thing about European nations: They can't hate
you so bad they wouldn't use you.

RB: Mar. 31, 1935

*"I never go to Detroit
without seeing Henry Ford,"
Will Rogers wrote.*

29

Here is Russia with twice our national resources, three times our size, bending every government energy to throttle all religion. All you have to do is look at the two countries and see who's policy is the best.

DTII: Mar. 4, 1930

Diplomats are just as essential to starting a war as Soldiers are for finishing it.

You take Diplomacy out of war and the thing would fall flat in a week.

ML: Jun. 9, 1928

I don't care how little your country is, you got a right to run it like you want to. When the big nations quit meddling then the world will have peace.

DTIV: Aug. 9, 1933

Military Service

You know lots of people in Europe wondered how America could train men so quick. Well, when you only have to train them to go only one way you can do it in half the time.

WAI: Jul 8, 1923

I think the best insurance in the world against another war is to take care of the boys who fought in the last one. YOU MAY WANT TO USE THEM AGAIN.

WAI: Dec. 30, 1923

Well, they brought our Soldiers back from Germany last week. Would have brought them back sooner but we didn't have anybody in Washington who knew where they were. We had to leave 'em over there so they could get the Mail that was sent to them during the war. Had to leave 'em over there anyway; two of them hadn't married yet.

WAI: Feb. 18, 1923

You promised them [veterans] everything but the kitchen stove if they would go to war. Now a lot of our wealthy men are saying, "Oh, I am willing to do anything for the disabled but nothing for the well." It wasn't these boys' fault they didn't get shot. (I don't see them doing anything for the SICK.) When he went away you didn't tell him he had to come home on a stretcher before you would give him anything, did you?

WAI: Dec. 30, 1923

War and Peace

You know you can be killed just as dead in an unjustified war, as you can in one protecting your own home.

WAIV: May 26, 1929

I tell you wars will never be a Success until you do have a Referee, and until they announce before they start just what it's for.

WAI: Jan. 21, 1923

There ain't nobody on earth, I don't care how smart they are, ever going to make me believe they will ever stop wars.

WAI: Jul. 22, 1923

You got to trust aviation in war. Why can't you trust it in peace?

DTI: Dec. 11, 1928

In fact, every war has been preceded by a peace conference. That's what always starts the next war.

WAI: Jul 22, 1923

Peace is like a beautiful woman — it's wonderful, but has been known to bear watching.

DTII: Nov. 3, 1929

People talk peace, but men give their life's work to war. It won't stop till there is as much brains and scientific study put to aid peace as there is to promote war.

DTII: May 31, 1929

Disarmament

Well, the [disarmament] conference met today and appointed a commission to meet tomorrow and appoint a delegation who will eventually appoint a subcommittee to draw up ways and means of finding out what to start with first.

DTII: Jan. 28, 1930

Now, there is nothing that makes a nation or an individual as mad as to have somebody say, "Now, this is really none of my business, but I am just advising you."

They never will get anywhere with this disarmament, for no nation can tell another nation what they need to defend themselves. That's a personal affair.

If I sleep with a gun under my pillow, I don't want somebody from across the street to "advise" me that I don't need it.

DTIII: Sep. 21, 1932

*Will Rogers tries out
the first gear-shift Ford
off the assembly line,
a gift from Henry Ford in 1927.*

Preparedness

We are the only nation in the world that waits till we get into a war before we start getting ready for it.... Pacifists say that "if you are ready for war, you will have one." I BET YOU THERE HAS NOT BEEN A MAN INSULTED JACK DEMPSEY SINCE HE HAS BEEN CHAMPION.

WAI: Aug. 10, 1924

Ammunition beats persuasion when you are looking for freedom.

DTIII: Sep. 19, 1931

"Draft capital as well as men." Any time you take everything that every man has got the same as conscript, Boys, there ain't going to be no war.

WAI: Jul. 22, 1923

Our army played our navy Saturday and the game was refereed by our aviation students, both good men. We will have a football team from our aviation school as soon as our far-sighted statesmen appropriate enough to have eleven students. They are just waiting for two more wars to see if flying machines are practical.

DTI: Nov. 28, 1926

34

Civilization Hasent Done Much But Make You Wash Your Teeth

Progress

Those were great old days, (but darn it any old days are great old days. Even the tough ones, after they are over, you can look back with great memorys.)

WAVI: Jun. 2, 1935

We will never have true civilization until we have learned to recognize the rights of others.

WAI: Nov. 18, 1923

What spoiled China was somebody saving their History. The minute you teach a man he is backed up by Tradition, why, you spoil him for real work the rest of his life.

ML: Apr. 2, 1932

The present generation don't know what a milestone is. They go by so fast nowadays that miles mean nothing.

WAI: May 18, 1924

Clowning in his costume backstage,
Will types his "Will Rogers Says..."
column on a Western Union blank
as Harry Hershfield watches.

We are just stepping too fast. In the old days we figured the world owed us a living, now we figured he owes us an Automobile, a Player Piano, and Radio, Frigid Air, and Clara Bow. The Automobile is to take you places you would be better off if you dident go to. The Player Piano is to discourage you from trying to play your own simple little tunes that your folks spent so much on your learning. The Radio is for Pepsident. The Frigid Air is too give you ice water when you would be better off if you dident load up on it, and Clara Bow will just lead you plum astray. She will give a Country boy the wrong impressions.

WAIV: Aug. 24, 1930

A liberal is a man who wants to use his own ideas on things in preference to generations who, he knows, know more than he does.

WAI: Feb. 4, 1923

We are living in an age of "urge." We do nothing till somebody shoves us.

DTII: Feb. 25, 1931

There is nothing that sets a nation back as far in civilization as prosperity.

DTIV: Apr. 2, 1933

Civilization has taught us to eat with a fork, but even now if nobody is around we use our fingers.

WAVI: Jan. 20, 1935

Women

During this reign of indigestion I was called on to speak at a big banquet at the Waldorf to the Corset Manufacturers. Now that only shows you what a degrading thing this after dinner speaking is...

This speaking calls on a fellow to learn something about articles that a self-respecting man has no business knowing about. So that's why I am going to get away. If a man is called on to tell in a public banquet room what he knows about corsets, there is no telling what other ladies' wearing apparel he might be called on to discuss. So me back to the morals of Hollywood before it's too late.

WAI: Mar. 4, 1923

You know, there ought to be some kind of a star given to any woman that can live with a comedian.

RB: May 11, 1930

I'll bet you the time ain't far off when a woman won't know any more than a man.

WAI: Apr. 29, 1923

They first showed us their calves. Well that looked fairly promising, and we seemed enough shocked to add spice to our views. But when they just practically overnight yanked another foot off their apparel and we woke up one morning with thousands of knees staring us in the face, why there is where I will always think they overstepped and took in too much territory.

WAIV: Apr. 20, 1930

Mothers are the only race of people that speak the same tongue. A mother in Manchuria could converse with a mother in Nebraska and never miss a word.

RB: May 11, 1930

Just passed by one of our fine country clubs out here and there was a big crowd there. It was the woman's golf championship of

America. We used to think going to see women play golf would be like going to see men crochet, but say, there is nothing effeminate about this golf thing as played by these champion women.

DTII: Oct. 17, 1930

You see short dresses was made for certain figures, but fashion decrees that everybody be fashionable, so that means there is going to be folks try and keep up with fashions that while they might be financially able are physically unfit, their purse is good but their build is bad.

WAIV: Apr. 20, 1930

Miscellaneous

I have always noticed that any time a man can't come and settle with you without bringing his lawyer, why, look out for him.

WAI: Jan. 14, 1923

Men are gradually realizing that a thing that is free is of no earthly importance.

WAI: Apr. 27, 1924

You wire the state or the federal government that your cow or dog is sick and they will send our experts from Washington and appropriate money to eradicate the cause. You wire them that your baby has the dyphtheria or scarlet fever and see what they do.

WAI: May 11, 1924

Say there ain't no civilization where there ain't no satisfaction, and that's what's the trouble now, nobody is satisfied.

WAIV: Jan. 5, 1930

A debt is just as hard for a government to pay as it is for an individual. No debt ever come due at a good time. Borrowing is the only thing that is handy all the time.

DTII: Mar. 1, 1931

I have always felt that the best doctor in the world is the Veterinarian. He can't ask his patients what is the matter — he's got to just know.

E: p. 10

Actual knowledge of the future was never lower, but hope was never higher.

Confidence will beat predictions any time.

DTIV: Sep. 19, 1933

There was more money spent on hogs' sickness by state and federal government than there is on children, when one child's life is worth all the hogs and cows that ever had a disease. If you want the government to help you don't tell them it is any human sickness. Tell them it is boll weevil or chinch bugs, and they will come a running, because they have big appropriations and men paid for that.

WAI: May 11, 1924

Great artists say that the most beautiful thing in the world is a little baby. Well, the next most beautiful thing is an old lady, for every wrinkle is a picture.

RB: May 11, 1930

Of all the cockeyed things we got in this country at the present time, it's some of our judges, and courts, and justices.

We got more bandits out on bond than we got people for 'em to rob.

DTII: Dec. 18, 1930

Did you read how many thousands (not hundreds) but thousands of students just graduated all over the country in law? Going to take an awful lot of crime to support that bunch.

DTIII: Jun. 15, 1931

(Scientists) can tell you just to the minute when something is going to happen 10 million miles away and none of them has ever been smart enough to tell you what day to put on your heavy underwear.

WAI: Feb. 1, 1925

Golf is the only game in the world where it takes longer to explain than it does to play. You play it in 2 hours, and it takes the other 22 alibiing for what you didn't do.

WAI: Sep. 7, 1924

Yours for Cornbread, Chitlins and Turnip Greens

Why, in the good old days, they couldn't have fed you on your lap 'cause you couldn't have held all they would give you. Now you have to feel for it to find it.

WAI: Apr. 1, 1923

When you have helped to raise the standard of cooking, you have helped to raise the only thing in the world that really matters anyhow. We only have one or two Wars in a lifetime but we have three meals a day. There is nothing in the world that we do as much of as we do eating.

Fashions in Beverly Hills Foods, 1931 Foreword

You know a man with a message is a whole lot harder to listen to than any other species of speaker. That is why I recommend Chili. It's the only thing I have ever found that will strengthen a man up to listen to all he hears.

WAI: Jun. 24, 1923

There is a little Chili joint on Broadway and 47th Street where there is just a counter and a few stools, but...what chili!

WAI: Jun. 24, 1923

Will Rogers visits his friend,
John D. Rockefeller, in Florida.

Chili...would be a Godsend for those Rotary, Kiwanis and Commercial Clubs.

WAI: Jun. 24, 1923

Going to have beans for supper tonight...navy beans cooked in Oklahoma ham, raised on the Dogiron ranch at Oologah, Cooked plenty soupy like. Got to eat 'em with a spoon, raw onions and corn bread, nothing else. Anybody that would want anything else ought to be shot.

WAVI: Feb. 25, 1934

Yours for corn bread, chitlins and turnip greens.

DTI: May 15, 1927

No Wonder
You See More People
at a Circus
than at a Church

If they are going to argue religion in the church instead of teaching it no wonder you see more people at a circus than at a church.

WAI: Jan. 20, 1924

Our Savior performed some pretty handy feats in the early days and his exploits have been handed down through the ages and made him our greatest hero, all accomplished without the aid of a newspaper.

WAIV: Jul. 24, 1929

That's one trouble with our charities, we are always saving somebody away off, when the fellow next to us aint eating.

DTIII: Mar. 22, 1932

Whoever wrote the Ten Commandments made 'em short. They may not always be kept but they can be understood. They are the same for all men.

WAVI: Mar. 17, 1935

Will Rogers sometimes caught a nap when he sat down to read the papers.

Hunt out and talk about the good that is in the other fellow's church, not the bad, and you will do away with all this religious hatred you hear so much of nowadays.

WAI: Mar. 11, 1923

Statistics have proven that there are twenty-five bathtubs sold to every Bible.

WAI: Apr. 1, 1923

Charity is the only way to help all these different kinds of people. Anyhow, if you are going to do anything at all for 'em, feed 'em, even if they don't become Christians.

ML: Apr. 30, 1932

The preacher started reading his prayer, which was new to me. Where I come from if a man can't think of anything to pray about offhand, why, there is no need of him praying.

CA: Jun. 11, 1924

I bet any Sunday could be made as popular at church as Easter is if you made 'em fashion shows too. The audience is so busy looking at each other that the preacher just as well recite Gunga Din. We will do anything, if you must in some way turn it into a show.

DTIV: Apr. 22, 1935

They were very religious people that come over here from the old country. They were very human. They would shoot a couple of Indians on their way to every prayer-meeting.

WAVI: Jun. 10, 1934

Will Rogers spread laughter over the air
during the dark Depression days.

There is no argument in the world carries the hatred that a religious belief does. The more learned a man is the less consideration he has for another man's belief.

WAI: Jan. 20, 1924

I have sometimes wondered if the preachers themselves have not something to do with this. You hear or read a sermon nowadays, and the biggest part of it is taken up by knocking or trying to prove the falseness of some other denomination. They say that the Catholics are damned, that the Jews' religion is all wrong, or that the Christian Scientists are a fake, or that the Protestants are all out of step.

Now, just suppose, for a change they preach to you about the Lord and not about the other fellow's church, for every man's religion is good. There is none of it bad. We are all trying to arrive at the same place according to our own conscience and teachings. It don't matter which road you take.

WAI: Mar. 11, 1923

Just Load in Your Kids
And Just Start Out

Travel

But if you want to have a good time, I don't care where you live, just load in your kids, and take some congenial friends, and just start out. You would be surprised what there is to see in this great Country within 200 miles of where any of us live. I don't care what State or what town.

WAIV: Aug. 31, 1930

There ought to be a law against anybody going to Europe till they had seen the things we have in this country.

DTII: Aug. 14, 1930

Columbus discovered a new World, but the old Tin Lizzie has made us discover America.

HT: p. 123

With Mrs. Will Rogers (Betty)
are their three active youngsters,
Jim (in the tree), Will, Jr. and Mary.

Tourists

A bunch of American tourists were hissed and stoned yesterday in France, but not until they had finished buying.

DTI: Aug. 2, 1926

I had visited some strange places in the world, but it was always so full of Tourists by the time I got to it that the Tourists were stranger than the place.

WAIV: Apr. 14, 1929

Winter is coming and tourists will soon be looking for a place to mate.

DTIII: Oct. 27, 1932

Traffic

The only way to solve the traffic problem of this country is to pass a law that only paid-for cars are allowed to use the highways. That would make traffic so scarce that we could use our Boulevards for children's playgrounds.

WAI: Jan. 6, 1924

1907, in Chicago, they built bumps in the roads to keep autoists from speeding. This custom has been followed out faithfully in most cities ever since.

WAI: Jan. 18, 1925

Places

Oklahoma is the only one of the three (Florida, California, Oklahoma) that has an all-year-around Climate. Our people don't move with the seasons, hunting a different climate. Our climate changes with our seasons. Why, we throw away more climate that we don't need in one year than you have charged your customers with! We don't sell climate; it goes with the purchase of land, just as the darkness or the light. We don't have to throw in a Gulf Stream or a trade wind or a canceled state income tax or a movie contract or a catfish. There are no remnant sales in Oklahoma. California has to irrigate, Florida has to fertilize. Now it seems hardly right, does it, that the Lord would take both those off an Oklahoman's hands? We don't have to depend on a dam; nor Chile for nitrates. You just throw anything out in Oklahoma and all you have to do is come back and harvest it.

HT: May 29, 1926

I think the time will come when everybody will be made to stop off at Claremore on their way to any place they may be going.
WAI: May 25, 1924

You know, if you have lost any one, look out here [California], because sooner or later they will come here to visit relatives, for anybody that has relatives comes here so he can write back to the other relatives.
WAI: Sep. 16, 1923

...Tulsa, Oklahoma, which would have been a real town, even if its people weren't greasy rich with oil, for it is founded on the spirit of its people.
WAI: Jul. 22, 1923

Canada. They have truly been a good Companion; I won't call 'em Neighbors, for they havent borrowed enough from us to be called Neighbors; I would prefer to still call 'em Friends.
ML: Feb. 27, 1932

Been interested in the scheme of my old friend Jack Garner of Texas. Jack wants to divide up the great State of Texas into five states. Why he wants to stop at five nobody knows. If he is going to split the old open range up, why not make a job of it.

WAIV: Jun. 8, 1930

Ah, say, fly over a Big City at night! Daytime is like slumming compared to seeing a big lighted City from the air at night.

HT: Jan. 28, 1928

Cities are like gentlemen, they are born, not made. You are either a city, or you are not. Size has nothing to do with it.

DTIV: Apr. 30, 1934

If you think Texas ain't some size you just try to drive from one part of it to another.

DTII: Jan. 27, 1931

Of all the airports I have been in Tulsa leads. In fact, they lead the entire United States with 4,500 passengers handled last month. We are putting in a field here in Claremore but we have to move fifteen or twenty blocks of big buildings.

DTII: Sep. 20, 1929

Mr. and Mrs. Will Rogers

You Can Always Joke About a Big Man

You know I have often said in answer to inquiries as to how I got away with kidding some of our public men, that it was because I liked all of them personally, and that if there was no malice in your heart there could be none in your "Gags," and I have always said I never met a man I dident like.

WAIV: Jun. 29, 1930

This thing of being a hero, about the main thing to it is to know when to die.

Prolonged life has ruined more men than it ever made.

DTI: Jul. 17, 1928

Cowardice or Bravery is never racial. You find both in every Country. No country has a monopoloy on Bravery; great deeds of heroism is liable to break out in the most unexpected places.

ML: Mar. 12, 1932

It's not what you pay a man but what he costs you that counts.

WAII: Mar. 22, 1925

Hurrah for Mr. Rockefeller, 96 years old today, one of the very few men that knew how to give money away so that every dollar does good.

DTIV: Jul. 8, 1935

51

The old fellow (John D. Rockefeller, Sr.) looks like he is extremely happy and satisfied, and I think that he has been of some service to his Country as well as to the passing Motorist. He has not only filled the Country's tanks, but has filled many a diseased man with hope of a cure.

Then it's the lesson he has been to other rich men. We all have a good deal of Sheep in us. If somebody does something, we are awful liable to jump over the same place he did. So it's his lesson to other rich men, and that has made them more liberal. Now we have hardly any great rich man that has not some form of Charity that he is extremely interested in. They know that to just be rich in this Country is no longer any novelty. It's not the wealth they had that we remember, it's what they did with it.

WAIV: Jul. 20, 1930

I just last night wrote a letter to Helen Keller telling her how fortunate it was she couldn't see me — and they don't make them much more remarkable than Helen is.

RB: May 11, 1930

A lot of wise guys have had a lot of fun joking about [Henry] Ford because he admitted one time that he didn't know history. He don't know it — but history will know him! He has made more history than his critics has ever read.

RB: Jun. 1, 1930

Why, if our youths followed you, Colonel [Charles Lindbergh], they would all be in the Atlantic Ocean. I have two boys. I want

Noted pilot Charles Lindbergh piloted his friend, Will Rogers, from San Diego to Los Angeles in 1927. Both men were heroes of the decade.

them to admire you, but I don't want 'em trying any of these stunts that you are pulling around here. I want the boys with me a while yet.

ML: Jun. 9, 1928

America and the whole world mourned Will's passing in 1935 and missed his daily column in the morning newspapers.

Cities Are Born,
Not Made

Cities are like gentlemen, they are born, not made. You are either a city, or you are not. Size has nothing to do with it. New York is "yokel" but San Francisco is "city" at heart.

DTIV: Apr. 30, 1934

Policemen here in New York, where the impression of some out of town people seems to be that nobody in New York cares for anybody else! There is not a day that you don't read of the wonderful things performed by them and the firemen to save human life. I tell you it does your heart good to read these things, even if we haven't got the nerve to be in on it, ourselves.

WAI: Feb. 15, 1925

There is only one trouble with New York, and that is that it is the most self-centered place in the world, outside an Englishman's London. It feels like it's the biggest place in the world and ought to run everything, but it just don't. Politically, nationally, it just looks like Claremore, Oklahoma.

HT: Oct. 29, 1927

There is twenty Golf courses nearer New York than any flying field they have and it takes less ground to land on than to make a golf course on, yet the biggest City in the World has no regular place to land. You lose more time getting into the city than you save by flying there.

HT: Jan. 28, 1928

I know how proud Christopher Columbus must have felt when he heard they had named Columbus, O., after him.

DTII: Feb. 16, 1930

Every State in the Union gambles as much as Nevada does, but they were smart enough to pass a law and get some tax money out of it. If Wall Street paid a tax on every "game" they run, we would get enough revenue to run the government on.

DTIII: Mar. 20, 1931

Nevada — it's freedom's last stand in America. Yet they don't do one thing that other states don't do.

Only they leave the front door open. You can get a divorce without lying, a drink without whispering and get on a game of chance without breaking even a promise.

DTII: Aug. 31, 1930

When you are laying out your European trip this Spring, don't overlook the Old Emerald Isle. It's got 'em all beat for beauty, romance, humor and hospitality, and the best horses in the world.

DTIII: Mar. 17, 1931

Well, here we are in Tucson, the champion humane town of America. Its climate has prolonged more people's lives than any single place. It has a fine university, and the best college polo team in the U.S. This up-to-date little city is just situated near enough to Mexico to get a touch of liberty.

DTIII: May 8, 1931

Carlsbad Caverns is just the Grand Canyon with a roof over it.

Then, when you get inside it's got all the cathedrals of the world in it, with half of 'em hanging upside down.

DTIII: May 10, 1931

Don't miss seeing the building of Boulder Dam. It's the biggest thing that's ever been done with water since Noah made the flood look foolish.

You know how big the Grand Canyon is. Well, they just stop up one end of it and make the water come out through a drinking fountain.

DTIII: Sep. 6, 1932

Brazil ought to belong to the United States. We like to brag about everything "big."

We been flying up its coast line for five solid days and still got another day.

If any of you see the Rockefellers, kiss 'em for me. There is not a mosquito up this coast....

Rio Janerio is the prettiest city in the world from the air. We are circling Para where we land for the night. It's right at the mouth of the great Amazon River.

DTIII: Oct. 24, 1932

I was here [New England] last week during the celebration of "Patriot's Day," that's a thing they just have up here. It has something to do with the time when the English overestimated their fighting qualities and they started a Revolution. Well that's the time Paul Revere unhitched an old Buggy Horse, jumped on him bareback and announced, "This is Paul Revere broadcasting from Bunker Hill Station, shut off your sets and grab a musket. The British are coming and if they don't stop to get tea they are liable to be here any minute."

WAIV: Apr. 28, 1929

I see where Mr. Hoover got a great welcome in Nicaragua. No wonder. I guess he and Lindbergh were about the only Americans they ever saw that weren't marines.

DTI: Nov. 28, 1928

I always told you that there was just three towns in the whole of America that was different and distinct, New Orleans, Frisco and San Antonio. They each got something that even the most persistent chamber of commerce can't standardize.

DTIII: Nov. 4, 1931

This Alaska is a great country. If they can just keep from being taken over by the U.S. they got a great future.

DTIV: Aug. 13, 1935

The Japanese are a good race of people in a lot of ways. We may just as well admit it; we can't compete with them when it comes to work. A clock and a bed are two things that a Jap farmer never used in his life.

WAI: May 4, 1924

I have been in twenty countries and the only one where American tourists are welcomed wholeheartedly by everybody is in Ireland...They don't owe us and they don't hate us.

DTI: Aug. 1, 1926

Tourists, you are missing something if you don't visit Washington while the politicians are not here. You have no idea the difference it makes....Why, if they could get this Capitol moved away from here this would be one of the best towns in America. I think there are people in this city smart enough to vote.

DTI: Aug. 26, 1927

I like Ireland and Mexico better than any other Countries. They both got humor, and while they both think they take life serious, they don't. They will joke with you, sing with you, drink with you, and, if you want, fight with you — or against you, whichever you want — and I think if they like you well enough they would die with you.

ML: May 19, 1928

I also have no humorous cracks about Mexico being lazy. If they are any lazier than us, which I doubt, but if they are, and can make a living at it, why, then I give them credit of being the smartest Nation on earth. For our own educational system is to teach our youth to learn something so that he will feel assured he won't have to do any manual labor through life. So if Mexicans can abstain from physical work without having to go to school 12 or 14 years to learn how not to work, then I claim that's a national asset.

ML: May 19, 1928

Say, what a City this is! She (Mexico City) is a cross between New York, Tulsa and Hollywood, with a bit of Old San Antonio and Nogales, Arizona, thrown in.

ML: Jun. 9, 1928

Well, I have been stepping pretty fast since I last dropped you a line. These Japanese! Now, here is something I better tell you right off the reel: Don't ever call a Japanese a "Jap." Now, I dident know that till I got over here; I just thought that it was about like Englishmen calling us "Yanks"; even if you come from Alabama, the English don't know but what you are a Yank just like Mr. Coolidge. But this Jap business is a serious matter with them.

ML: Mar. 12, 1932

These Japanese run their Wars just like they do their trains — right on time.... War is a business with these folks. When a War shows up, they don't have to stop and put in a Draft and sing songs, and make three-Minute speeches, and appoint Dollar-a-Year men. All that has been attended too long before the War ever broke out. All their Soldiers are trained between Wars — not after one starts.

ML: Mar. 12, 1932

Now, about you Filipinos and your Freedom? Do you really want your Freedom, or do you just want to Holler? Personally, I believe a Country can get more real joy out of just Hollering for their Freedom than they can if they get it.

ML: Apr. 30, 1932

I dident know before I got there and they told me all this — that Rome had Senators. Now I know why it declined.

L: 1926

(Las Vegas) It's a dandy little city and you'll hear much of it, for it's only fifteen or twenty miles from the site of the great Boulder Dam that will eventually be built when the Government takes it over and tells each state what they get instead of what they want. It has to be built, for the Lord has already done most of the work, and this very Las Vegas is the place that will be the headquarters of all the work and workmen. You will see this name in many a date line in the next few years.

HT: Jan. 21, 1928

Arrived Canada capital today. More sentiment here to be annexed by Mexico than by America. They know us too well. If we get any nation to join us it will have to be some stranger.

DTI: Oct. 11, 1926

Ireland treats you more like a friend than a tourist.

DTI: Sep. 8, 1926

I have seen today some of the most beautiful stock farms in America. I don't think there is another place in this country quite like the blue grass region around Lexington . . . They know how to scramble a bran mash for a horse and a corn mash for a human that just about excels any hospitality in America.

DTI: Jan. 15, 1927

Canada is a mighty good neighbor and a mighty good customer. That's a combination that is hard to beat.

WAV: Aug. 28, 1932

Well, here we are in Newport. In flying from New York we flew low here over the beach and beautiful homes. That's one way they can't keep the riffraff from looking in. If this exclusiveness looks to me like a good thing I am going to take it back and introduce it in Beverly Hills. We screen folks won't let a mere millionaire land in our town, but Newport is a great old place. If you are not a sailor or a millionaire you feel out of place here.

DTI: Jul. 23, 1928

Roswell, N.M. . . . this is the prettiest little town in the West.

DTIII: Sep. 23, 1931

Well that was some trip. Thousand-mile hope from Seattle to Juneau. Nothing that I have ever seen is more beautiful than this inland passage, by either boat or plane, to Alaska.

DTIV: Aug. 7, 1935

South Bend, Ind. I always wanted to see this town. I was born in a Studebaker wagon, awakened every morning by a Big Ben clock, grew up walking between the handles of an Oliver chilled plow, wore home made shirts made by Singer sewing machines and read all my life of Notre Dame.

DTI: Nov. 29, 1926

Hershey, Pa. If I knew your your address I would send you some fine chocolates. This is the cleanest and best run town I ever saw.

DTI: May 30, 1927

Lima, Ohio . . . this is the biggest bean town in the world.

DTI: Nov. 24, 1926

Battle Creek, Mich. . . . what a place this is. The home of the sensitive stomach.

DTI: Apr. 3, 1928

Been traveling today down through the beautiful Shenandoah Valley of Virginia — and boobs are leaving to see Europe!

DTI: Apr. 29, 1927

Arizona . . . and New Mexico . . . are different from all other states . . . They have a romance in history that out dates anything we have in our whole country, and there is just enough Indians to keep the whole thing respectable.

WAV: Jan. 1, 1933

Say, if you want to visit the most beautiful country in the United States, don't overlook these Ozark Mountains.

DTI: Feb. 22, 1927

You don't have to be warlike to get a real kick out of our greatest army post, Schofield Barracks, and the navy at Pearl Harbor. If war was declared with some Pacific nation we would lose the Philippines before lunch, but if we lost these it would be our own fault.

DTIV: Aug. 1, 1934

Colorado is our grand stand seat to see the world from.

WAV: Jan. 1, 1933

Minneapolis has always been one of my pet cities, they have been good to me on every occasion I was ever there.

WAV: Jan. 8, 1933

Nogales, Arizona, it's what Western towns used to be but it still is.

DTIV: Mar. 26, 1933

You would love Nevada. It's the West without dressing up to look the part.

DTIV: Mar. 22, 1934

Well you actors and politicians can have all the race horses and cigars and perfume named after you, but I got some clippings from down in South Carolina that was mighty gratifying to me.

Will Rogers, an old pot hound, was voted the best hunting dog in the State, and he took another prize for the finest looking dog. So my regards to the champion of South Carolina.

DTIV: Nov. 12, 1934

Vice-President John Nance Garner enjoys a cigar and a visit with close friend Will Rogers in October 1933 at Uvalde, Texas.

63

Big Smoky Mountain Park . . . it's going to be the Yellowstone of the South. It's beautiful and can't help from being a big success as a public park for tourists.

DTI: Mar. 7, 1928

Aimee Semple McPherson's daughter is in the Ozarks and the Arkansawyers notified her that she was welcome but that they didn't want to be "redeemed, saved or liquidated."

That's right, too. There is pretty strong characters down there. You can't redeem 'em, you just join 'em. That's what I had to do about 27 years ago with one of 'em. . .

Anytime you tangle with an Arkansaw hillbilly or hillbilly-ess, you are going to run second.

DTIV: Jul. 30, 1935

Seattle is a real city, the end of the main line, New York in miniature, boats from China, Japan, Los Angeles seven hours by plane, Spokane, Minneapolis, and Chicago by plane. Sixty lakes are in sixty-minutes drive by car from City Hall.

The Lieut. Governor of the State is a fiddle player, the only politician in America with a legitimate profession.

DTIV: Aug. 6, 1935

California

Frisco is one of the only three distinctive cities left in the United States which was built, not just assembled. San Antone and New Orleans are the others.

DTII: Mar. 7, 1930

Everything is in California, all the great sights of nature, and along with all these wonders we have out here is the World's greatest collection of freak humans on earth. We maintain more freak religions and cults than all the rest of the world combined. Just start anything out here and if it's cuckoo enough you will get followers.

WAIV: Dec. 8, 1929

Breezing along over the snowcapped mountains of Northern California. Breakfast in Beverly, dinner in Seattle. There is nothing more beautiful in America than looking down on this redwood highway.

DTIII: Nov. 19, 1931

Now Barnum invented the tent, but Billy Sunday filled it. He can get more people into a tent than an Iowa picnic at Long Beach, California.

WAI: Sep. 16, 1923

This town is going through a "wild orgy" of bridge building. You daren't leave a few buckets of water out overnight or somebody will build a bridge over it by morning.

DTIV: Aug. 5, 1935

The Catalina Island that this fellow Wrigley has stuck together in the Pacific is an American garden spot. Every gum chewer should visit it. You swim, golf, fish and chew.

DTII: Nov. 27, 1930

The Mayor of Beverly — The Claremore, Oklahoma, of the West Coast.

DTI: Dec. 26, 1926

Eighty-two years ago today California entered the Union, on a bet...would eventually be called California and not America.

We took it away from Mexico the next year after we found it had gold.

When the gold was all gone, we tried to give it back, but Mexico was too foxy for us.

It's a great old State; we furnish the amusement to the world; sometimes conscientious, sometimes unconscientious, sometimes by our films, sometimes by our orators, but you can't beat it.

DTIII: Sep. 9, 1932

California always did have one custom that they took serious, but it amused the rest of the United States. That was in calling everything a "ranch." Everything big enough to spread a double mattress on is called a "ranch."

DTIII: Aug. 30, 1932

Oklahoma

I, myself, belong to the Oklahoma Society in New York. We meet every year in a member's single room at the Mills Hotel — all four of us. Now judge for yourself which is the best State.

WAI: Jan. 28, 1923

... Tulsa (a residential suburb of Claremore, where we park our millionaires to keep them from getting under our feet).

WAI: Feb. 24, 1924

...(Claremore, Oklahoma, greatest one night stand health resort in the world).

WAI: Nov. 11, 1923

Now my home is Claremore, OK., the home of the best curative waters in the world and, by the way, one of the best towns in the world to live in if any of you are thinking about making a change.

WAI: Feb. 24, 1924

We have all kinds of various "weeks" — "Eat an apple week," "Don't shoot your husband week," "Don't cuss the Republicans any more than you can help week."

But, Claremore, Okla., the home of the great radium water, is having this week one of the most practical and useful ones, "Take a bath week." Even the Rotarys, Kiwanis, Lions, Apes, and Chamber of Commerce have joined in the novelty of the thing and it bids fair to become a yearly event.

DTIII: May 27, 1931

If Oklahoma does in the next twenty-two years what we have in the last, why New York will be our parking space, Chicago our arsenal, New Orleans our amusement centre and Los Angeles segregated for Elk and Shrine conventions.

DTII: Sep. 18, 1929

When you are visiting the beauty spots of this country, don't over-look Frank Phillips's ranch and game preserve at Bartlesville, Okla. It's the most unique place in this country.

DTII: Sep. 22, 1929

Breakfast in Beverly and dinner in Claremore. These are two cities we been needing to have joined by a regular passenger line.

The town is so crowded here we have to put our airport in the edge of Tulsa, and that Tulsa and Claremore airport broke a world's record in May just past. They hauled 10,212 passengers.

DTII: Jun. 6, 1930

Well, overnight, in order to get our great Oklahoma pilot, Post, and his famous partner, Gatty, to come there, they just tore down and blasted out blocks of homes, and now they got the best landing field in the world (outside of the Templehof Field in Berlin) just ten minutes' drive from the heart of Claremore.

DTIII: Jul 8, 1931

Oologah, Okla., my real old home, had a fine celebration Saturday. Sure sorry couldn't make it. Unemployment is terrible, but employment is worse.

DTII: Oct. 26, 1930

The South (Oklahoma) is dry and will vote dry. That is, everybody that is sober enough to stagger to the polls will.

DTI: Oct. 28, 1926

Played this morning at the best agricultural school in America, Oklahoma A. and M. Their cattle win all the shows, and their boys win all the judging contests. It's not a racoon coat college.

DTII: Feb. 5, 1931

Just flew in from Chicago. Was going over to Claremore tonight, but the hotels are all so full, going to have to stay here in the edge of town [in Tulsa].

I see where some line is going to make aviation pay by taking it out of the pilots' salary. When they start hiring cheap pilots I will stop flying.

DTIII: Feb. 19, 1932

Pawhuska and Tulsa people used to come over to Claremore for their mail and to find out what time it was. We had a clock there.

RB: Apr. 20, 1930

Say, you talk about a city, this Buenos Aires is as big as Chicago, as live as Paris, beautiful as Beverly Hills and as substantial as Claremore, Okla.

DTIII: Oct. 18, 1932

Oklahoma, Al Smith is coming down there tomorrow, and I want the old home to treat him right....Show him the State produces something besides outlaws, bo-weevil and comedians.

Tell him what a great territory we had before we struck oil and Republicans, followed by mortgages, foreclosures and impeachments.

DTI: Sep. 18, 1928

Just flew over Oklahoma City, where they have struck the big oil wells right in town. They are going to move the Capitol buildings to put in wells. State and Federal capitols have ruined forty-eight towns and cities in this country. No town has ever survived a capitol, so, as I see it, to strike oil is the only salvation.

DTII: Sep. 22, 1929

Well, this week just passed has been pretty busy in New York. It looked like my home town of Claremore, Oklahoma, on a Saturday afternoon.

WAI: Jan. 21, 1923

I am writing this in the Navy "Hell Diver" at five thousand feet, and just landing at Stillwater, Okla. for a ten o'clock morning show. The best A and M College in America.

WAIV: Feb. 15, 1931

Oklahoma is a doubtful State, and after hearing all the candidates on both sides, it's still doubtful what good any of them will be to it.

DTI: Oct. 26, 1926

On my way home to Oklahoma. What's happier, especially if people have forgot what you used to be?

DTI: Jun. 3, 1927

Claremore, Okla. is just waiting for a high-tension line so they can go ahead with locating an airport.

DTII: Aug. 29, 1929

See where a lot of cities are kicking on their census, blaming the government because they haven't got more people. Claremore, Okla., come through with a 254 gain. That's not per cent, that's people. Folks make towns, not numbers.

DTII: May 12, 1930

You see the Lord in his justice works everything on a handicap basis. California having the best of everything else must take a slice of the calamaties (earthquakes). Even my native Oklahoma (the Garden of Eden of the West) has a cyclone. Kansas, while blessed with its grasshoppers, must endure its politicians. New York with its splendors has its Wall Street, and Washington, the world's most beautiful city, has a lobbyist crawling out to attack you from every manhole....So every human and every place is equal after all.

DTIV: Mar. 12, 1933

There is a good deal in the papers about giving my native state of Oklahoma back to the Indians. Now I am a Cherokee Indian and very proud of it, but I doubt if you can get them to accept it — not in its present state.

When the white folks come in and took Oklahoma from us, they spoiled a mighty happy hunting ground....

WAI: Jan. 27, 1924

We are the Chamber of Commerce of Claremore, Oklahoma, the town that needs no introduction to an intelligent audience.

HT: May 29, 1926

Claremore Oklahoma is the only one of the four unique Cities that has retained its individuality. When progress hit us we dident go cuckoo. We are a town that can stand prosperity without letting the newer element lose their heads.

HT: Unpublished article, p. 152

All I know is what I read in the Claremore Progress. Towns booming, fine aeroplane field all lighted, Oklahoma Military Academy best polo team in the country.

Claremore is the flowered city and the exilirating odor of roses are entrancing. The sweetest smelling town in the U.S.

DTIV: Apr. 2, 1935

This is a great old Town, if you like old Towns. Personally, I like new Towns. Tulsa, twenty years ago, was my idea of a real City. 'Course, it's aged now, kinder like Peking. But when she was new and had no Tradition, she was a hummer.

ML: Mar. 19, 1932

Restless America is looking for a new place to fix the tires, and we are here to announce to the half-witted rovers of America that Oklahoma has been designated by Nature as the parking place of the last and greatest boom.

HT: May 29, 1926

Oklahoma is the heart, it's the vital organ, of our national existence.

HT: May 29, 1926

Claremore, Oklahoma, a town that reached its enviable position through hard work, perserverance, and water that will cure you of everything but being a Democrat.

HT: American Magazine, Apr. 1929

Oklahoma has the greatest Wild West performers in the world. We have produced more ropers and less Cabinet members than any state in the Union. Visitors will enjoy our interesting Indians. They will see the Osages dressed in nothing but a Rolls Royce car.

HT: Unpublished article, p. 150

As for the distance from New York, that means nothing to us. Let New York estimate their distance from us. We make no effort to toady to their millionaire trade. We raise our own millionaires in Oklahoma.

HT: May 29, 1926

I have toured and looked over every city in the United States in the past year, and I think Tulsa is the livest, most progressive one, with the exception of Claremore, in the United States. It's the hub of the Oil Industry, so every Realtor should study Tulsa. If your state or city ever strikes oil you will know how an oil city should be conducted.

HT: Unpublished article, p. 149

This Ada sounds like a girl, but it's not. And it's not a town; it's a city.

DTI: Oct. 22, 1926

In the nation's capital to film "A Texas Steer" in 1927, Will Rogers pretends to go fishing near the Washington Monument.

Live and Let Live
And Laugh This Thing Off

Philosophy

You got to sorter give and take in this old world.
WAIV: Jun. 1, 1930

You must not condemn a people until you have been among them and can second know their angle.
DTI: Oct. 16, 1926

What constitutes a life well spent? Love and admiration from your fellow men is all that anyone can ask.
WAII: Aug. 9, 1925

Well, anyhow, we are living in great times. A fellow can't afford to die now with all this excitement going on.
WAVI: Jun. 30, 1935

A man that don't love a horse, there is something the matter with him.
WAI: Aug. 17, 1924

So let's be honest with ourselves and not take ourselves too serious, and never condemn the other fellow for doing what we are doing every day, only in a different way.
L: 1926

I admire any man that can rise above his surroundings.

RB: May 18, 1930

That's all there is to success is satisfaction.

WAIII; Jul 29, 1928

Nobody wants to be called Common People, especially common people.

WAII: Jun. 21, 1925

No man is great if he thinks he is.

DTI: Mar. 1, 1929

You got to sorter give and take in this old world.

WAIV: Jun. 1, 1930

But it's only the inspiration of those who die that make those who live realize what constitutes a useful life.

DTIV: Mar. 7, 1933

Discontent comes in proportion to knowledge.

WAIV: May 11, 1930

We elevate ourselves but we should never reach so high that we would ever forget those who helped us get there.

Speech on Scribner, Jan. 14, 1925

There is nothing as easy as denouncing. It dont take much to see that something is wrong, but it does take some eyesight to see what will put it right again.

WAVI: Jul. 28, 1935

You can't broaden a man's vision if he wasent born with one.

WAIII: Apr. 22, 1928

Us ignorant people laugh at spiritualists, but when they die they go mighty peaceful and happy, which after all is about all there is to living, is to go away satisfied.

DTII: Jul. 7, 1930

You can't have a picnic lunch unless the party carrying the basket comes.

DTIII: Jan. 21, 1932

The Lord so constituted everybody that no matter what color you are you require the same amount of nourishment.

WAIII: May 8, 1927

Nothing makes a man broad-minded like adversity.

DTIV: May 5, 1933

It's great to be great but it's greater to be human.

DTII: Feb. 28, 1930

When the judgment day comes, civilization will have an alibi "I never took a human life, I only sold the fellow the gun to take it with."

DTII: Jul. 15, 1929

Now rumor travels faster, but it don't stay put as long as truth.

WAI: Mar. 9, 1924

Everybody is ignorant, only on different subjects.

WAI: Aug. 31, 1924

Human Nature

…nobody can fall out and get as sore at each other as kin folks.

DTIV: Nov. 23, 1934

The minute a fellow gets into the Chamber of Commerce he quits mowing his own lawn.

WAI: May 20, 1923

I don't care how smart you are, if you say something you are liable to say something foolish and the smarter you are, and the longer you talk the more fool things you will say.

WAI: Aug. 24, 1924

The more people study about you, nowadays, the less they think of you.

WAI: Jun. 3, 1923

There ain't nothing that breaks up homes, country and nations like somebody publishing their memoirs.

DTIV: Dec. 23, 1934

There ain't but one thing wrong with every one of us in the world, and that's selfishness.

DTIV: Mar. 10, 1935

Well, we cuss the lawmakers. But I notice we're always perfectly willin' to share in any of the sums of money that they might distribute.

RB: Apr. 7, 1935

The boy on the sand lot gets just as big a kick out of a home run as Babe Ruth.

WAIV: Oct. 26, 1930

No man can be condemned for owning a dog. As long as he's got a dog he's got a friend and the poorer he gets the better friend he has.

WAIII: May 8, 1927

It's terrible to have a law telling you you got to do something. But you ain't going to do it unless there is.

DTIV: May 31, 1935

There is quite a difference. When you are worried you know what you are worried about, but when you are "confused" it's when you don't know enough about a thing to be worried.

DTIV: Apr. 23, 1933

Popularity is the easiest thing in the world to gain and it is the hardest thing to hold.

RB: May 18, 1930

If you want to know how a man stands go among the people who are in his same business.

WAI: Sep. 28, 1924

A Ford car and a marriage certificate is the two cheapest things there is. We no more than get either one than we want to trade them in for something better.

RB: Jun. 1, 1930

It's awful hard to get people interested in corruption unless they can get some of it.

WAIII: Apr. 22, 1928

So buy a ranch somewhere in the West. All your life every man has wanted to be a cowboy. Why play Wall Street and die young when you can play cowboy and never die?

DTIII: Jul. 10, 1931

Everybody nowadays is suggesting ways of getting prosperous on somebody else's money.

DTII: Feb. 17, 1931

Funny thing about human nature. When we ain't feeling so good ourselves, we always want to read about somebody that is worse off than we are.

DTII: Dec. 9, 1930

A fanatic is always the fellow that is on the opposite side.

RB: Jun. 8, 1930

Society

You know, when you have to be told what to say when you meet anyone, you are not the one to meet them.

ML: Jan. 8, 1927

Culture, after all, is nothing but studied indifference.

ML: May 19, 1928

What is Tradition? It's the thing we laugh at the English for having, and we beat them practicing it.

ML: May 26, 1928

I doubt if a charging elephant, or a rhino, is as determined or hard to check as a socially ambitious mother.

DTIII: May 10, 1932

I often wonder how they distinguished a Gentleman in the old days when there was no Golf.

WAI: Jan. 21, 1923

You know there is a great tendency all over the country now to be High Brow. Everybody is four-flushing and pretending they are not what they really are, especially here in New York. More people should work for their Dinner instead of dressing for it.

Half the stiff bosom Shirts worn nowadays, the Laundry is due on them yet.

There are men belonging to swell Golf Clubs today, who, if their Wives ever wanted a Cook, would faint. Their dues are paid before the grocery bill.

WAI: Feb. 25, 1923

Holidays

Every holiday ought to be named "Labor Day." If we could ever get vacations down to where you wasn't any more tired on the day one was over than on our regular work day it would be wonderful.

DTIV: Sep. 4, 1933

I propose a Father's Day. No flowers, no fuss — just let him use the car himself and go where he wants to. But we will never live to see such a contented day.

DTII: May 11, 1930

Newspapers

I hope we never live to see the day when a thing is as bad as some of our newspapers make it.

DTIV: Jul. 19, 1934

Any person that don't read at least one well-written country newspaper is not truly informed.

DTIII: Jul. 27, 1932

But with all its faults the old Paper is our daily bread. Sometimes it's burned, and sometimes not cooked to suit us but we got to have it everyday and its intelligence is always in keeping with its readers.

WAIV: Nov. 23, 1930

We are living in an age of publicity. It used to be only saloons and circuses that wanted their name in the paper, but now it's corporations, churches, preachers, scientists, colleges, and cemeteries.

DTIII: Jun. 23, 1931

We don't give our criminals much punishment, but we sure give 'em plenty of publicity.

DTIV: Feb. 2, 1934

After all, most prominent men have sensible sides if you can only get their mind off themselves and the humor of their importance.

WAI: Nov. 30, 1924

Every gag I tell must be based on truth. No matter how much I may exagerate it, it must have a certain amount of truth.

WAI: Mar. 9, 1924

Memoirs — ...means when you put down the good things you ought to have done, and leave out the bad ones you did do.

ML: Mar. 12, 1932

The Salvation Army is proof of how respected and useful an organization can get if you keep it out of politics.

DTIII: Aug. 21, 1932

For when I write 'em (articles) I am through with 'em. I am not being paid reading wages. You can always see too many things you wish you hadent said, and not enough that you ought to.

WAIV: Sep. 1, 1929

Miscellaneous

I have always noticed that people will never laugh at anything that is not based on truth.

WAI: Nov. 30, 1924

I have always maintained that one profession is deserving of as much honor as another provided it is honorable.

WAI: Aug. 17, 1924

Education

History ain't what it is; it's what some Writer wanted it to be.

ML: Mar. 11, 1932

There is nothing as stupid as an educated man if you get him off the thing he was educated in.

WAV: Jul. 5, 1931

You know I believe the Lord split knowledge up among his subjects about equal after all. The so-called ignorant are happy. You think he is happy because he don't know any better. Maybe he is happy because he knows enough to be happy. Well, the smart one knows he knows a lot, and that makes him unhappy because he can't impart it to all his friends. Discontent comes in proportion to knowledge.

WAIV: May 11, 1930

Viva Hooey!

Yours for truth, even if it interferes with news.

DTI: Aug. 22, 1926

Yours for the lowdown on public servants.

DTI: Nov. 26, 1926

There is no way to stop this country. Just quit listening to the Politicians...The Constitution will remain as is. The Russians are not going to take us.

WAVI: Jul. 14, 1935

Viva diplomacy, nobody is fooled, nobody is hurt. Viva Hooey.

DTIV: Oct. 8, 1933

*Will flashes a big grin for his fans
as he accepts a king-size wooden lock to the city
from New Orleans Mayor Arthur O'Keefe (far right).
Rogers toured the country, raising funds
to benefit flood victims, in 1927.*

*Will Rogers entertains a weary
Democratic Convention
at the Chicago Stadium
in June 1932.*

ABBREVIATIONS

Selections are from the writings of Will Rogers,
as published in the 22-volume set
by Oklahoma State University and
the Will Rogers Heritage Trust.

E	*Ether and Me, or "Just Relax"*
BS	*There's Not a Bathing Suit in Russia & Other Bare Facts*
ID	*The Illiterate Digest*
PC	*The Cowboy Philosopher on the Peace Conference*
P	*The Cowboy Philosopher on Prohibition*
L	*Letters of a Self-Made Diplomat to His President*
CA	*Convention Articles of Will Rogers*
DTI	*Daily Telegrams: Volume I, Coolidge Years, 1926-1929*
DTII	*Daily Telegrams: Volume II, Hoover Years, 1929-1931*
DTIII	*Daily Telegrams: Volume III, Hoover Years, 1931-1933*
DTIV	*Daily Telegrams: Volume IV, Roosevelt Years, 1933-1935*
WAI	*Weekly Articles: Volume I, Harding/Coolidge Years, 1922-1925*
WAII	*Weekly Articles: Volume II, Coolidge Years, 1925-1927*
WAIII	*Weekly Articles: Volume III, Coolidge Years, 1927-1929*
WAIV	*Weekly Articles: Volume IV, Hoover Years, 1929-1931*
WAV	*Weekly Articles: Volume V, Hoover Years, 1931-1933*
WAVI	*Weekly Articles: Volume VI, Roosevelt Years, 1933-1935*
HC	*"He Chews to Run": Will Rogers' Life Magazine Articles, 1928*
ML	*More Letters of a Self-Made Diplomat*
HT	*"How to Be Funny" and Other Writings of Will Rogers*
RB	*Radio Broadcasts of Will Rogers*

"Live your life
so that whenever you lose
you are ahead,
Will Rogers stated
as his personal philosophy

WAV: Jul 30, 193